T0380826

BELIEVE

in the

POWER OF YOU

ANTHONY BELGRAVE DIXON

To order additional copies of this book, contact:
Xlibris
1-888-795-4274
www.Xlibris.com
Orders@Xlibris.com

ISBN: Softcover   978-1-7960-2072-4
       EBook   978-1-7960-2073-1

Print information available on the last page

Rev. date: 10/07/2019

This book is dedicated to everyone out there struggling to
find themselves, my mother Jacqueline Belgrave Dixon
whose strength flows within me,
my grandmothers Angela Belgrave and Lynette Walker,
and all the beautiful strong women who showed me
unconditional love and help shape me into the man
I am today, you know who you are.
THANK YOU!
and most importantly to myself for never giving up on me.
Believe in the Power of You.
Thank you to the islands of Barbados and San
Blas, Panama for their picturesque beauty.

BELIEVE
In The
POWER
Of YOU 🤍

Sometimes it's not the devil, it's the decision.

*** "My destiny has not been written yet, I do not resign myself to my fears. I dare to live my dreams, I dare to be great." ♥ ♥ ♥

Your apology needs to be as loud as the disrespect was.

God only allows you to be rejected by what doesn't matter to your destiny.

Your wound is probably not your fault but
your healing is your responsibility.

When life gets crazy.... have a cup of tea, get dressed up
and go to a boss ass party, surround yourself with people
who genuinely love you ♥, listen and learn from those
who inspire you, eat whatever u want, look at yourself
in the mirror, laugh, and remember that the person
looking back at you hasn't and never will leave your side
so don't give up on him or her ♥ xxo You're Beautiful!

How do you expect the universe to help you
if you don't believe it can happen?

Believe in what you pray for

Dear Universe,

Today's word is PLAN

My PLAN is to gain financial freedom, security, and abundance from sources of creativity that not only benefit me but all those who surround me as well. What is your PLAN?

If you ask God for patience, Does God give you patience or an opportunity to be patient? Same goes for COURAGE, STRENGTH, LOVE… etc. Be aware of the opportunities that present themselves each and every day to do exactly what you've been praying for.

Sometimes you fall off the wagon for months... Sometimes you say you're going to start fresh on Monday and by Wednesday you've already fallen back off... Change is a process, Sometimes you have to restart 100 times and it's frustrating... but you will be ok, ♥ I promise! Just don't give up on yourself ... one day at a time ♥

Success doesn't change you... Fame
does. -Whitney Houston ♥

Everybody's out here trying to be Insta-
Famous... Miss me with that shit,

I just want to be successful and achieve everything I dream
with my eyes closed… Realized with my eyes open ♥

Friends would laugh at me because I don't have
a car…. I've never wanted a car… I've always
wanted a boat! ♥..... Soon come…

Throughout your day and everyday THINK of these 6 things:

Something that made you Happy,
Something that brought you peace,

Something that made you smile,
Something that made you laugh,

Something that made you feel beautiful,
Something that made you feel sexy.

#<u>Repeat</u>

God Give me the Courage I need to Step Outside of my Comfort Zone! Search my ♥ and Reveal to ME where I've been Holding Back and Playing it Safe! Give ME Definite Guidance on the Actions you want me to Take so I can See my Life moving in a Powerful way! Please don't ever Stop Flowing through me. ♥ ♥ ♥

Don't let the idea of love ♥ have you thinking
that it is love. ♥#LoveTakesTime

Same goes for success... just because you had a taste
of it doesn't mean you've arrived. ♥ ♥ ♥

Don't cry over boys.... do some squats and make
them cry wishing they still had that ass!!!!

Love the life you lead, live the life you love... for tomorrow is not promised to anyone ♥ ♥ ♥ in a world filled with darkness be somebody's light.

Gods got me covered... ♥ and for that I am forever Grateful.

Not all storms come to disturb you...
Some come to CLEAR your path.

Choose to win.

I'm a Believer in Peace and Love ♥… But I say FUCK a lot! You either get bitter or you get better… It's up to you to choose.

Never Stop, Nevah Sekkle #BelieveInThePowerOfYou

The biggest struggle for woke people, is living in a world full of sheep, where everyone around you is saying bahhhh when they should be fucking howling!! But you can't nyam the dead there's no substance ... Stay strong!

Let's just put it out there and speak it into existence…
I will have it All Because ALL is already within me.

Don't settle for less just because it's available.

If you're stressed because your plate is full........ Think back and remember what it was like when you were starving.

If you see your glass as half full... pour that
shit into a smaller glass! Bet it's full now
#YoureWelcome ♥ Believe in the Power of You.

3 simple rules in life. If you do not go after what you want, you will never have it. If you never ask, the answer will always be no. If you do not step forward you will always be in the same place.

Everybody is trying to launch their business
but nobody's taking a business class.

Everybody is trying to live their dreams
but nobody's putting in the investment.

Everybody is saying they're the next best thing
but didn't study or even know who came before them.

Unless Kris Jenner is your mama or you
got that Kardashian money...
Bitch! Study your craft!!!

The only person you're fooling is yourself...
Just a thought!

It's that in between stage... knowing what's coming and the realistic goal of when you can really start to make it happen.... It's in that stage of patience where recklessness and impatience can settle in and make it easy for you to lose your focus and knock you off track!! Keep your balance, own your life, let faith not fear guide you, and be prepared so when shit pops off you're ready!!!! Have fun, but remember.... This is what you've been waiting for..... Don't fuck it up!

It's a beautiful day to love yourself

Today, I am coming for EVERYTHING that is mine.
Everything that was once taken, everything not given, and
everything that I've missed. I'M COMING FOR IT TODAY.
I am coming for what belongs to me NOW. My money, my
love, my peace, my purpose, my dreams, my goals, my glory!!!

IT'S MINE. And I'm coming for it.

I believe I've earned it. I deserve it. I believe
I've worked for it. I believe I'm worthy. And I
believe that God has already said YES.

Dear God, I want ALL MY STUFF.
And I'm coming for it now.

I'm coming and you will deal! Matter of fact... I'm already here ♥ #Bloop

Wake up every morning and tell yourself you're a bad ass bitch from hell and that no one can fuck with you, and then don't let anyone fuck with you.

In this rat race through monotony and repetitiveness I yearn for longer bursts of excitement that set my soul on fire and my heart free! Where I can give back without question, set sails without worry, and be financially free to do whatever the FUCK I want!!!!! Still growing, Still learning, Still hustling, Still Believing ♥ #PatienceSimba

In 10 year's you will thank me, just hang in there ♥ ♥

I want it all... I will have it all… I've already got it all... it's all within me... I am worthy... I deserve it... I've got this... I am everything I choose to be.

Stop saying Yes to to the things you dislike, if you aren't feeling it... then you aren't feeling it! And that's ok ♥

Thinking of a Master Plan... Manifest your dreams
into reality... your best is yet to come.

You can't make excuses and money at the same time.

People with good intentions Make Promises…
People with good character KEEP THEM. And that's
the difference…though your intentions are good…
it's your character that doesn't sit well with me.

If u don't .... then who will ?

I think everything you want is being lined up for you ... if you've seized the opportunities and put the pieces in place... it's just a matter of hanging in there long enough to reap the harvest of your labor. What you put out will come back to you.... So many Great things have happened and are happening as we speak! #OverflowSeason #IJustWantASimpleLife ♥ Speak action into your life and water your soul with balance.

Time to get Uncomfortable!

The reason why a lot of people don't become who they want....
is because they are too attached to who they've been.
#ButIveAlwaysBeenThatWay ... how's
that working out for you?

I will not apologize for evolving past your comfort zone. Believe in the power of you and love yourself enough to give yourself the very best of you.

Whaaaaaat??? I can't hear you dear... too busy doing everything you thought I couldn't do.

If people are doubting how far you will go, go
so far that you can't hear them anymore.

Don't be distracted from your destiny trying to manage people's opinions. What they think about you is none of your business! The only people mad that you're living your truth are those in denial and/ or living a lie! #NoTime

Dust settles… I don't.

You are more powerful than you know, your roots run deep, you don't need the approval or understanding of others because you understand yourself! You are not your past, your past is simply a part of your journey, you are layered in growth and have risen from unbelievable depths. You defy limits, and shackles, and boxes, and chains. You are a beautifully mastered piece of art, multifaceted with talents. No one is like you, you are your own, you exist, you have purpose, you live, you love, you laugh, you are... You are Amazing and I love you!

Don't tell me the sky is the limit when
there's footprints on the moon.

Something will grow from all that you are
going through... That something is YOU!

The only person stopping you is... YOU! Get out of your own way and sip this tea.

Once I realized that my decisions were the cause for certain stress in my life I made better decisions.

It's a Beautiful day to start living your best life.

"it's not that they don't like what you're doing...
they just don't like that it's you doing it!"

I choose to be Unstoppable.

The Magic happens when you follow your heart.

Love didn't hurt you... Someone who didn't know
how to love ♥ hurt you. #KnowTheDifference

I never lose! I either win or I learn.

Some people aren't loyal to you... They are loyal to their need of you. Once their needs change... so does their LOYALTY! #BelieveInThePowerOfYouAndTellThatBitchBye

You need to align yourself with people who fit your destiny ♥ and not your history.

I didn't forgive you because you deserved forgiveness,
I forgave you in order to set myself free!

Your love ♥ language will be understood by those fluent enough to listen and reciprocate it. It's not your duty to teach people how to love ♥ you!

Believe in the Power of You ♥ Don't stop for
nobody but God, Own EVERYTHANG!!!!

New day, New week, New vibrations, New
money, New tingzzzz. #LetsGetIttttttttttt ♥

What you seek is also seeking you ♥ Patience, don't give up.

Do what gives you Peace.

Fall in L♥VE with someone who will never let you fall asleep wondering if you still matter. Fall in love with yourself.

It's a beautiful day to take another step closer to your dreams.... If the universe wants you to have it then you will! And if not, then the universe will direct you to something bigger and better ... just believe and push through.

You don't learn to un-love them ... You just learn to love yourself more.

And then I realized what I truly wanted...
and it was simple... Peace.

There's so much more to this thing called life, and if you don't get it.... trust me when i say…. someone else will!! And that my dear will be on you! ♥ I run my own race, I am in competition with no one, and yes I want it all!!!! Hopefully you do too ♥

If you want to CHANGE what you SEE in
your LIFE..... YOU must first CHANGE
what you BELIEVE in your MIND.

Know the difference between those who stay to feed
the soil and those who come to grab the fruit.

If you're waiting for someone to save you...
you best look in the mirror dear.

There will always be someone who can't see your worth ... don't let that someone be you dear!

We repeat what we don't repair.

Don't stop dreaming just because you had a nightmare.....
go back to sleep and fuck that bitch up!!!

I denied it, I meditated on it, I dismissed it, I ate lentils and veggies, I tried talking myself out of it, I prayed on it and then I remembered...... follow the flow of your life

Ahhhh that's nice..... Don't be afraid to lose people... Be afraid to lose yourself trying to keep them in your life! ♥ ♥ People need to learn how to save themselves... if you can't swim maybe it's time you learn gurrrrlllll!

You know gurrrrrllll ... sometimes giving someone a second chance is like ... giving them an extra bullet for their gun because they missed you the first time ... #StayWoke

If you're stressed because your plate is full........ Think back and remember what it was like when you were starving..

Keep Going .... You're almost there …

Because you deserve the best and owe
it to your God damn self!

Passion and Talent will only go as far as your Work Ethic
🖤#PutInTheWorkSeeTheResultsAndKeepGoing 🖤

What a Beautiful Dream.

One day I WILL have a million dollars in the bank!! 1 million, all mine ♥ ♥ #ThereISaidIt 1 MILLION!!!

Are you living? …. No, but i mean really.. ARE YOU LIVING? If you were gone tomorrow would you consider that a life that was lived… or did you simply exist amongst the living? LIFE is short… fuck it up a little bit, jump outside the box, laugh a lot, see the world, let the world see you, don't take any shit you don't deserve, and get it ALL ♥ ♥ ♥ Do you! Be you! And Live it up! ♥

If you woke up without a goal....
Go baaaaaaaaaaaaaaaaack to sleep!

Dream, Believe, Execute, Follow through, Repeat.

You will never have to force anything that is truly meant to be!!! ♥ That goes for everything in life.

You're going to be happy said life... but first... I will make you strong ♥

No one is YOU ... and that's your POWER!

Don't be so thirsty for success that you drink from every cup handed to you, same goes for love.

Being broke is part of the game, staying
broke is some personal shit.

Just because you want to see your people eat, it doesn't make you responsible to fix their plate.

Stop expecting LOYALTY from people who can't
even give you HONESTY ♥ #TruthHurts

What I know for sure is that... though people may not always be honest with you they are being truthful to their nature. Once you recognize said nature, habits, and or traits the only person you need to be honest with is yourself and choose what you will accept and reject from those people. If she / he is a crackhead then they are going to do do crackhead things.... that's it that's all #simple Don't fight them with your expectations and feelings of being let down.... she/ he is a crackhead darling, it doesn't mean they're a bad person it just means don't be surprised if you invite them over and your wallet goes missing, same thing goes for hoes!

Be the change you want to see in yourself ♥ Stop accepting, Stop settling, Stop making excuses for yourself and for others... Allow yourself to just be.... And be GREAT!

You're about to enter a season of consecutive wins... ♥
You can't bring everyone with you and that's ok! As you
stick to your values and pursue your sense of purpose
let 0 FUCK$ be given to those who stand in the way
of achieving your dreams or disrespect your love!

I will not apologize for evolving past your comfort zone.
#NotMyProblemNorMyResponsibility

Stop giving CPR to dead situations. You can lock a zombie in the basement all you want but as soon as you get too close or that shit breaks free it's going to bite you!

Stay out the mix, Stay low, Get money, Stack, Stack some more, Eat good, Travel, Do different shit, Pop out every now and then.

"They threw dirt on my name but didn't realize I was a seed! The bricks they threw at me I used to stand on and further strengthen my foundation. When they abandoned & disregarded me... I became my own team and lead myself to victory.

When they said I couldn't do it..... I did!!! #YouGotThis ♥

Here's what I know for sure…. if you don't do it, then somebody else will. There is no relevance in could've, should've, would've. At the end of the day it's either YOU did or YOU didn't!!! 🖤

Something will grow from all you are going through and it will be you. Stop beating yourself up about it and just handle it! Just because the leaves fall off a tree doesn't mean the tree is dead, weak, any less beautiful, or dying. Sometimes things need to fall to replenish what's within and create new growth boo. Still STRONG, Still STANDING, Still GROWING, Still PRESENT! Love you some YOU boo!

Trust The Journey, Respect The Process,
Spread Love 🖤 I want it all!

Your life on this earth is EVERYTHANG, OWN IT!!!! love it, nurture it, grow it, be it, do it, live it. ♥ ♥ ♥ The ONLY person in your way is you!! Change your mindset, brainstorm the plan, find your balance, own your evolution, give love, give back, and give to yourself #BigLove #GoodLife if you are not happy with where you are in life.... you don't have to stay there!! Stop choosing the lie, recognize the truth for what it is and act on it!! ♥*** "My destiny has not been written yet, I do not resign myself to my fears. I dare to live my dreams, I dare to be great."

Your new life... is going to cost you your old one. #LetItMarinate #BeReadyForChange

Though the devil does try my faith cannot be shaken and my God never leaves my side. ♥ I've had setbacks, i've faltered, i've lost my way, i've suffered great loss, i've been without food, without money, without a home, without work, through hell and back again, and through it all i remain standing, i remain here, and i refuse to give up. Life is beautiful and precious, keep pushing towards your dreams, indulge in the things you love, and learn the lessons from both negative and positive experiences. Embrace your authentic self and know that you are not made to be perfect, you are made to love with your heart and be you. Everything you want will happen for you, you just got to go through the process, and believe me It's a motherfucking process, but YOU ARE WORTH IT!

#DREAMBIG #DONTGIVEUP #LIVELOVELAUGH #EVERYDAYSANEWDAY ♥ ♥ Bless

You are more powerful than you know, your roots run deep, you don't need the approval or understanding of others because you understand yourself! You are not your past, your past is simply a part of your journey, you are layered in growth and have risen from unbelievable depths. You defy limits, and shackles, and boxes, and chains. You are a beautifully mastered piece of art, multifaceted with talents. No one is like you, you are your own, you exist, you have purpose, you live, you love, you laugh, you are .... You are Amazing and I love you, ♥ ♥

Some people just aren't ready for you, and that's ok.

Anything that annoys you is teaching you patience. Anyone who abandons you is teaching you how to stand on your own feet. Anything that angers you is teaching you forgiveness and compassion. Anything that has power over you is teaching you how to take your power back. Anything you hate is teaching you unconditional love. Anything you fear is teaching you courage to overcome your fear. Anything you can't control is teaching you how to let go.

DAYDREAMING ♥ Love Yourself Enough To Simply
Let Go! Yes it is that simple! ♥ Replace the word Have
with Choose, you don't have to you choose to ♥ nothing
is easy but when you actively recognize your choices
the power to steer your destiny becomes easier.

Faith is the bridge between where I am and
the place that God is taking me.

A mistake repeated more than once is a decision.

To heal a wound you have to stop touching it.

You have to trust God at all times! The good times, the bad times, and the times when you don't know what to do. Trust God! Amen

God only gives 3 answers to prayer:
1. YES
2. NO
3. Trust me

I will not stop until everything I see with
my eyes closed... I have with my eyes open...
Don't stop for nobody but God xxo

Fall in love with yourself and own it!!! Own EVERYTHANG!!! ♥ LOVE all of you!! Not part of you all of it, because that's what makes you YOU, and that is your power!!

Sometimes you get the best light from a burning bridge... #NoTouchbacks keep moving forward, Believe in the Power of You!

i used to…. but i don't anymore….

Invest in yourself... You are your own best investment!

All you've got to do is dream, And Work Your ASS Off!!!! ♥

Accept the fact that some people didn't intend to let you down, their best is just less than you expected.

Because ultimately the choices you make are your own...
Be careful not to sabotage your dreams whilst chasing
opportunity! 🖤 #DreamBig#TrustTheProcess If you don't
build your dream, someone will hire you to help build theirs.

Mondayyyyyyyyyyy got me feeling like you choose how you want your day to start!!! U can whine and complain or you can throw on Toast by Koffee, buss it loud, twerk 2 times and go about your business!!

Fall in L♥VE with your LIFE!

You will. Always be disappointed when you expect people to act as you would! Don't get mad, get rich.

Trusssssst me... Greatness takes time ♥ And what's being created for you... Is just that Great! ♥ #YaBestBelieve

Let's be real ... You will never afford a yacht on minimum wage! You better step your standard up of what you're willing to work for, get your skills in check, and that hustle gurrrlll! #DreamBigAndGetYaMoneyUp

You have to walk towards the things that keep you Alive
Just do it.... You will thank yourself later!

One Dream at a time…

Take Ownership! It sucks sometimes, but THAT'S life ... Sometimes life will FUCK you and you just gotta change positions and find some way to enjoy it! Own your Mistakes, Own your Lessons, Own your Achievements, Own your Decisions, Own your Dreams, Own your Direction, Own your Life. Just FUCKING! Own it!! ♥ And Love you some YOU TODAY!!! #BelieveInThePowerOfYouuuuuuuu

It's a Beautiful day to invest in your Dreams ♥
♥ #OneThingAtATime YOU got this!

It's not really work when you're doing what
you love ♥ ♥ keep pushing for the things
you love and watch your world change.

It's funny how those who threw dirt on your name be mad when flowers grow out of it! Only to try and come back into your life and reap the harvest on some "Heyyyyy long time no see..." #ByeFelicia God said: Because of where I am taking you, there are people from your past coming back to you, be careful, I've already shown you who they are.

Never be ashamed of a scar... It simply means you are Stronger than whatever tried to hurt you.

I think it's important to realize that you can miss something,
But NOT want it back! #DidntTheyTellYouThatiWasASavage

Never let small minds convince you that
your DREAMS are too big!

Stop giving the same person different
opportunities to disappoint you
#AintNobodyGotTimeFaDatUnlessYouMyChild ♥ xxo

Let it marinate ♥

Work hard
Fail
Fail
Fail again
Keep working at it
Believe it will happen
Then allow yourself to win
#YouDeserveThis ♥

It's the little things that remind you of purpose and just how beautiful life is.

The only person who can affect change is you ♥ Don't be too hard on yourself ... It's a process. Greatness takes time, trial, and error ♥ You Got This!!!

Having just one key to the city just isn't enough,
I want them All!!! I don't knock Bitch,
I Enter!!! #NuffSaid 🖤

You want 50k likes on Instagram.. I want 50k in a duffle bag ... Trust me we are not the same or compatible boo boo xxo #GetMoney 🖤

Dear God,

Thank you for the changes that are occurring in my life. Thank you for releasing my blessings and opening doors I didn't know existed. I release my fears and let go of my worries. I trust you. I believe in you. And I will boldly walk through those doors with faith, authority, and love. I am ready.

Amen...

Be the change you want to see there is no right or wrong way there is just the way! 5+4=9, 7+2=9, 3+3+3=9, shall I continue... however which way you do it 2+4+1+2=9 just do it and eventually you will get there xxo 1+5+2+1=9

Own it!! Own it all! Your responsibilities, your lessons, your achievements, your growth, your opinions and ideals and decisions. Own your life ♥ ♥ Walk with purpose because you are worth it! Own it! Own it all!

The most Beautiful things grow from the deadliest of places. Don't be afraid to let some things die in your life so that some beautiful things can grow. Don't fight it just let it go. ♥

What's normal to the spider is chaos to the fly... Find your normal, don't nobody like flies anyway 🖤

Every great dream begins with a dreamer. Always remember, you have within you the strength, the patience, and the passion to reach for the stars to change the world.

~ Harriet Tubman

How do you expect anyone to reach out to
you if your arms are always folded?

Good luck with that!

I dont need your validation or for you to congratulate me, I congratulate myself everyday! #SelfLove Get into it! It took me a long time to get to where I am and if you think your petty side eye, why me, why not me emotions are going to affect that, think again fam. ♥ Live your life and keep my name out ya mouth until you're ready to grow up and reciprocate the love that I always gave to you.♥

Your not being ready is not my problem
nor my responsibility to fix. XO

If you're going to hang around dark clouded people then expect to get rained on. I like the sun way too much to stay in the shade, I might get the occasional downpour of rain every now and then ... But that's just to ensure that I keep growing. Xxo #GoodLuckWithThat ♥

Don't be frustrated by somebody else's perspective on how you do your shit, I've been told I do things backwards all my life, if how the way you do your shit brings you peace, clarity, and completion than that's what works for you darling! Don't let someone else's input or perspective taint your peace. Do you boo xxo #YourJourneyIsYourOwnDontGetConfused 🖤 🖤

Stop watering things that were never
meant to grow in your life.

If Today I left the house with 12 fucks and then came home with a dozen fucks, how many fucks did I give today?

Answer: 0 Fucks, I gave 0 fucks today. ♥ #NoFilter

Focus your mind on what you wish to create. ♥ There Ain't no shortcuts, trust the process for this dream, and this journey. This path is yours alone, so make it what you will. Choose to win and you shall. Xxo #Winning

Stop allowing people to give you their bare minimum!! If you let them get by on 60% levels then that's what they will continue to give.... And if after you communicated that to whomever and shit only goes up to 75% that's not an improvement that's bullshit, cut that fool off and see how quick they reach 100% levels #NoTime 🖤 It's simple accounting Hun .. If every time I chill with you and I give 100 and you give me 60 then I'm out 40 each time, meaning every time we chill my stock goes down... Bunn dat!!! #BunnYou #MoneyAhFiMek #LoveAndFriendshipAhFiBeReciprocated xxo

If haters want to throw bricks then let them, you've been building this foundation for years.... all they're doing is reinforcing its construction. 🖤 🖤

Flies like shit and sweet things...
#1 don't be shit!
#2 if you're feeling sweet set boundaries!

When people try to bring you down, it means you are already above them. Stay Bless xxo ♥ #AintNobodyGotTimeFaDat

It's not enough to believe and realize your dream, to keep it alive you must consistently work at it ♥

It may not be a competition for you but if you want to win at this most precious thing called

L I F E than you better get in the ring and challenge the Fuck out of yourself! Sitting on the sidelines watching life pass you by just isn't my cup of tea dear, to each their own though! Xxo ♥

Because you've got to be your own best friend!! Just because I don't confront you about it, doesn't mean I don't know you've been talking shit! We're grown now, ain't nobody got time for that or your bullshit excuses, live your life though! ♥ ♥ My time I give is an investment and if there ain't no returns on that, then it's time to sell stock darling! #MoneyAhFiMek #Simple ♥

I'm a L ♥ V E this life till there ain't no more life in me! Xxo #LiveItUp

Live Your Life For You ♥ ♥ give back, love a lot, try new shit, learn new shit, Love yourself, make money, live your passions, shake off the bullshit, keep reaching, don't stop for no one but God, Believe in you!!!!!!♥ #YouGotThis#DontQuit xxo ♥ #DreamBig ♥

THE END
PURA VIDA!!!

NOTES:

BELIEVE
In The
POWER
Of YOU 🤍

NOTES:

BELIEVE
In The
POWER
Of YOU 🤍

NOTES:

BELIEVE
In The
POWER
Of YOU 🤍

NOTES:

BELIEVE
In The
POWER
Of YOU ♥

NOTES:

BELIEVE
In The
POWER
Of YOU 🤍

BELIEVE IN THE POWER OF YOU!